A
COUNTRY
ALPHABET

Heather Tanner

Robin Tanner

A
Country
Alphabet

HEATHER &
ROBIN TANNER

The Old Stile Press

Special Edition: ISBN 0 907664 04 0
Main Edition: ISBN 0 907664 05 9

PREFACE

The making of an alphabet book was Nicolas McDowall's inspiration, born inevitably of his passion for the printing press. When we first visited him he had just acquired one cherished specimen, a Columbian of 1854, and already the entire family were sharing his enthusiasm, helping to set the type for greetings to friends, experimenting with papermaking.

By the time we could travel again to Blackheath the Columbian had proliferated. The car was back in the garage from which it had been ousted, and a handsome press room had been built in the garden for the Columbian and its seven companions, ranging from ancient giants which Caxton would have had no difficulty in using to the latest arrival whose simple appearance belied its efficiency. For one delightful game or another all might be, and are, used.

We had been hardly surprised therefore when Nicolas came up with the suggestion that Robin should design an alphabet of capitals two inches high decorated with country things, each contained within an area of about five by four inches and occupying a page. On the opposite page, Heather would write to complement the drawing.

Robin as designer needed no invitation to play with letter forms, nor Heather to muse on her favourite theme of the miraculous birth of language, in which the whole Tower of Babel, still unable to intercommunicate, had found it expedient to build its utterances with single units, letters with individualities and names of their own.

It proved an enjoyable, light hearted enterprise. The only problem was to choose among the possible images for each design, and many were the discussions over the offerings - abstruse, ridiculous or impossible - before the decision could be made. The summer heat kept Robin at work in his cool studio. As a drawing was finished Heather would contemplate it as she went about the daily chores, now and then scribbling an idea on the nearest piece of paper. Meanwhile Nicolas was trying out types, working out pagination, choosing paper. We all - very much 'all', with the indispensable help of the two households - were ready more or less simultaneously.

INTRODUCTION

What a strange fossil is this our alphabet that still keeps its Greek name; first picture-writing, then signs for sounds, then tools for word-making; and now, long divorced from phonetics, responsible for surely one of the world's most inconsistant of orthographies. Who established its sequence? Why does it start with 'A'? the first sound uttered when we come into the world? There is an order: the vowels progress from front to back palatal, and are rationed out among the consonants roughly one to every four or five, while the more rarely used letters huddle together at the end.

Infants must of course learn their letters - do they still have to learn the alphabet by heart? Fortunately it lilts along in a trochaic quatrain:

> A b C d E f G
> H i J k L m N
> O p Q r S t U
> v W X y Z.

And said backwards it even rhymes:

> Z Y X and W V
> U T S and R Q P

ONM and LKJ
IHG, FED, CBA.

Although no longer hieroglyphs or runes, the symbols have re-acquired personalities of their own, christened with an extra sound before or after to make them pronounceable - Eff, Dee, Jay, and how about Aitch? Moreover, through the centuries a succession of Pygmalion sculptors, scribes and typographers have got to work on them, until by now each reader and writer has his own conception, his own favourites. I see my alphabet serried in a square as in some atavistic horn book, certainly not a memory of my very first book, painted for me by my father.

THE
ALPHABET

BY A CHILDHOOD TRADITION AS established as seasonal hopscotch, 'A' must stand for Apple, or Applepie. But for me it speaks of Appleblossom, pink and flocculent against a blue sky, bowed earthwards with the weight of years of fruit. In May the whole tree lights up with a scattering of carmine, then breaks into rose ever a little paler till the first rough wind scatters its snow. But each separate flower has all these hues too: red in bud, white open, or streaked and flushed with colour dark or pale, all perfumed with an elusive scent vaguely suggesting the apple-to-be; another delight, but the lesser. ❡ It calls up Samuel Palmer's Shoreham garden and Van Gogh's Provençal orchards; sentimentally too the old nursery oleographs of hushabye babies, cradled in appleblossom, while below them old Dobbins graze and little girls in white pinafores crown lambs with daisy chains. But because 'the first blossom is the best blossom' I return to the farms of home, where Robert Browning's chaffinch, that started to practise his happy notes on St Valentine's Day, is in full song 'on the orchard bough'.

Appleblossom

11

'B' MUST BE FOR BREAD, NO question. That is, the cottage loaf, whose shape it echoes. Why 'cottage'? The bread oven beside the cottager's open fire having limited space, a smaller ball of dough would top each lower one, the two pinned together by a dimpling thrust of a finger down the middle of both. ¶ And as old and as inevitable a craft was the making of Baskets, springing up all over the world in places whose peoples could never have met and taught one another, each basket-maker sitting on the floor, slightly raised so that his legs could spread comfortably before him, weaving first the circular base and then the uprights. ¶ Bearded Barley recalls Tennyson's 'reapers reaping early' who heard above the soft hiss of the corn that last sad song floating down the river to Camelot. Barley makes bread even more delicious than cottage loaves - but also harbours those tiresome little creatures called 'thrips', mere specks which settle in clouds in the hair of unfortunate local inhabitants. ¶ Festooning the picture is Black Bryony. By harvest time the quilted leaves are metallic and wine-dark, and its crowns and necklaces hung on hedge and tree are threaded with scarlet berries.

Basket, Barley, Bread, Bottle, Beet, Black Bryony

'C' IS A BEAUTIFUL LETTER, ALMOST an 'O' but not quite. It will be a sad day that banishes it as superfluous, for phonetically it is either 'K' or 'S' in our tongue. ❡ Imagine cowslip or cuckoo flower spelt with a 'K'! Cowslips no less than buttercups are (or were) 'the little children's dower', in blissful days of pre-conservation ignorance made into warm, soft, sweet-scented 'tisty-tosty' balls. Since then cowslips have been supplanted in the fields by unwanted barley, but are at last reappearing in an unexpected quarter - the motor-ways - as if nothing had happened. ❡ The German name, Himmelschüssel, is 'keys of Heaven'. The folk name 'paigle' is obscure, though there is a similar word for a measuring peg. Were they ever kept in a bunch? As children we called the hawthorn 'Peggy Iles', never asking why. The haws hang down in a bunch. Is there a connection? ❡ Country people seem to have called most Spring flowers 'cuckoo'. Shakespeare calls our cuckoo flowers lady's smocks 'all silver-white' - what a word for that washed-out lilac of the summer frocks that maidens bleached when daisies pied and violets blue painted the meadows with delight! A. E. Housman catches the echo in

littering far the fields of May
Ladysmocks a–bleaching lay.

Cowslip, Cuckoo flower

15

'AS OLD AS THE HILLS.' THE DOWNS seem the oldest, because they wear the oldest human documents - their dolmens and cromlechs and 'dismal cirques of Druid stones' which after four thousand years still elude interpretation. The very rock, shattered and shaped before man had evolved, was endowed by him with superhuman powers. That he was born with a touching instinct of immortality is revealed by his burial customs, Downland in stone chambers, Neanderthal in flowers. ¶ The Downs have a highly specialised flora, affected too by either overgrowing or overgrazing. It is in later summer that they come into their own, with thyme, eyebright, dandelions, salad burnet, restharrow, harebells and hawkweed near the turf; taller moondaisies, scabious, knapweed, marjoram; and on the hillocks felwort, centaury, yellow-wort, and pyramid and bee orchids. ¶ Early-evening is their best time, when slanting rays illuminate their soft sea-moulded contours, from the long line of distant crest, punctuated here and there by a semibreve of windbreak beechwood, to the velvet folds of golden-green falling steeply to the shadowed plain below.

Dolmen, Downland, Distance, Daisy, Dandelion

17

THERE IS ONE AUTUMNAL VISION
which the very young have never seen and the old will
never see again – the flicker of gold coins from the tops of
giant elms as they turn this way and that in their descent
to the golden carpet below. And it was the elm that would
usher in the year as well as close it, the crest lit with dark
red buds against a sky of storm-clouds. ¶ What a nightmare was the relentless spread of 'Dutch' elm disease!!
There are some hopeful regenerations, though they usually
give up, debilitated by the struggle. Attempts at cure
proved useless: was there prevention? Did anyone watch
that loading of infected timber and say nothing? Do we
preserve more woodland and plant more? ¶ Other trees
have come into their own to fill the spaces, but the elm
was special in so many ways, even though it could in a
gale not only shed a limb but be felled, its shallow spread-
ing roots taking the bank with it. But in summer its
massed foliage gave shade to cattle; in winter its fine skel-
etal shape provided windbreak, and as timber it will
endure for centuries, the beautiful grain giving
lasting joy.

English Elm

19

'F' IS A SOFT SOUND, A LITTLE LATE
to appear in the Aryan language, where it evolved from
an explosive 'p', made gentler by what physical or social
change? It should stand for such delicate things as feather,
feathery fescue grass, and feathery fern. To make the sound
the upper lip and teeth must bite the lower, as if faltering.
The very letter suggests it, upper member over lower! I
see my nineteen-ten schoolmates, each watching in fasci-
nated fright as the Mental Arithmetic question advances
inexorably down the line, to pause at last before her;
struck dumb, lips folded in embarrassment. ¶ Any no-
tion pressed too far in one direction collapses: beside fear,
fall, faint must be put ferocious, fight, fiend! Filberts are
hard, but properly start with 'Ph', being named after St
Philibert, whose day is August 22nd. ¶ Nothing could
be harder than a fossil - nor older. Man's puny threescore
years and ten shrink into eclipse compared with the count-
less millenia since this spiral swam in primitive oceans.
What kind of creature will find our fossilised remains,
and what will he make of them?

Fern, Filbert, Feather, Fossil, Fescue grass

GRAVEYARD. NO, DON'T TURN THE page: I want to write about it. 'God's acre'? Yes, if with a church (a cemetery is merely the undertaker's acre), where husband and wife lie in death as in life, in a double bed. On another tomb an unusual tragedy is revealed:

> *In bloom of life*
> > *She's snatched from hence.*
> *She had not room*
> > *To make defence,*
> *For Tyger fierce*
> > *Took life away,*
> *And here she lies*
> > *In bed of clay*
> *Until the Resurrection Day.*

Though it has an echo of Bottom's 'Pyramus', it was all too true a story. Who composed the verse? a relative of the little barmaid? a local poet? or the remorseful Malmesbury innkeeper who had rashly housed a travelling menagerie in his small back yard? ¶ There are pebble tombs near the east coast, millstone grit in the North, slate in Wales, and here the local Cotswold stone, golden weathered to grey. The drawing shows the gate leading to the vicarage, for the graveyard entrance is by lychgate. 'Lych' means 'body', not the self but merely its 'likeness'. He had the idea who made his epitaph: 'Received of Phillip Harding his borrowed earth. July 4, 1673.'

Gate, Grasses, Graveyard, & Gravestones

23

HAYMAKING USED TO BE THE SUMMER festival. It began with fields laid up for hay, white with moondaisies, rust and red with sorrel and clover, tinker-tailors and quaking grasses rippling into waves with every breeze. The weather would be watched for the right time to cut, to the clatter of horse-drawn machine and cries of 'Whoa!' After tossing, maybe many times, the hay would be raked into cocks and at last collected, forkfuls skilfully handed up from the loaded waggon to the still more skilful rickmaker. ¶ One may still see the craft in remote districts, in Ireland haycocks awaiting a dry day spread with large ineffectual handkerchiefs, in alpine terrain the hay furled with the tying rope into bales to be rolled down the mountainside. And still the branched limb of pliable wood – ash here, walnut in southern climes – is carefully selected to make that most functional tool, the rake. ¶ Otherwise the hay festival is no more. Admittedly that hard labour has also gone. But what has been substituted – crops 'scientifically' selected, sprayed, dried, stored – is a false alternative, at too high a price.

Hay rake, Haycocks, Hayricks, Honeysuckle

WHAT A LETTER! THE ONLY ONE TO be also a word - except 'A', which is only an 'article' and an indefinite article at that, whereas 'I' is so important that it must never be seen alone in lower case. 'I' must represent the dawn of selfconsciousness. It is common to all Indo–Germanic languages: ego, ich, je, I, are all ultimately the same word, little though they may look it. That single thin upright line suggests the uniqueness, the unassailability of each lone individual. ¶ 'Ivy' as a girl's name is comparatively recent, most popular at the turn of the century. Perhaps it grew from the Dickensian Christmas. The early Church in adapting the pagan winter festival had frowned on ivy as associated with Bacchanalian rites, but its willingness to be wreathed, the decorative quality of its varyingly marked leaves, oval or five-fingered, and its yearlong availability won the day. ¶ Some ancient prejudice may lurk in its undeserved reputation as a parasite: it depends on its own roots for food, climbing tree or wall by sucker pads till it is high enough above ground to flower - but may harm its host by overweighting, especially if itself laden with snow. The flowers are so late as to provide almost the last pollen meal for insects.

Ivy with natural variations

27

BESIDES THE HOUSEHOLD LARES
and Penates handed down the generations every member
of the family treasures some specially useful tool, and woe
betide anyone who mislays or misappropriates it. The jug
must have been such a favourite, for it won a pet name
which has replaced any ordinary name it ever had: 'Jug'
is an endearment for 'Joan', and belongs to the 'jack'
nicknames for handy instruments, up to today's motor-
car. There were 'jack' jugs too, usually of leather. ❡ A
jug to be found in every mediaeval kitchen, Dorsetshire
or otherwise, was the Verwood, the classic example of
basic Jug - swelling lower half of local clay baked to bis-
cuit colour, decreasing upper part yellow-glazed spout
pinched till it would pour, thumb pressure marks on the
handle that must balance it safely when full to the brim.
All other jugs can only be variations on the theme.
❡ Equally satisfying in design and beauty were the jars of
oatmeal-coloured pottery with eggshell glaze that could
once be bought with their contents. The shoulder, a draw-
back in a screw-top container was essential for tying the
parchment over the jam or jelly. How jammy 'jam' sounds
closing the lips with a smack, and how wobbly 'jelly'
sounds! though it once meant 'frozen' in its mould.

*Jugs (Verwood, Pleydell-Bouverie, Batterham) Jelly Mould,
Jam Jars, Wine Jar, two small Leach Jars*

29

EXCEPT IN FOLKLORE THE KINGCUP
and Queen Anne's Lace are the only royal flower names,
although the queen of Heaven is well commemorated –
Lady's Mantle, Lady's Bedstraw, Lady Fingers . . . and
Marsh Marigold, the kingcup's other name. Royal it
certainly looks, large, spectacular beside the cold streams
and ditches, deepest of yellows, shaped like a goblet.

O brave marsh marigold, rich and yellow,
Give me your money to hold!

cries Jean Ingelow's seven-year-old. ¶ They are Shakespeare's 'cuckoo buds of yellow hue', and also his 'mary-
buds' that 'begin to ope their golden eyes' with the music
of the aubade. The big 'blobs' (the country word) and
the flat plate-like leaves suggest the lily of garden pools.
So native are they to their watery home that they wilt
immediately when some intrepid wader snatches
at their gold.

Kingcup

31

I WONDER IF THOSE RELENTLESSLY
straight Roman roads were as much resented when they
were first made as motorways are now? They meant foreign
invaders, then armies, now juggernauts. For those wind-
ing tracks of early man had not been made by idle chance.
They would assuredly have run less indirectly had it been
possible, but there were streams to cross, woods and hills
to skirt, bogs to avoid, and on either side dykes must be
built for both shelter and cover. Once the horse was
domesticated tracks became roads, shared by both riders
and walkers. As walkers became riders, riders became
drivers, to whom no thoroughfare was sacred. ❡ A lane
is but the width of a waggon. It should be so unfrequented
as to grow grass down the middle. It is flanked by min-
gled hedges - 'hardly hedgerows, little lines of sportive
wood run wild', set in high banks covered in Spring
with primroses, celandines, stitchwort, ferns. Such are
lovers' lanes: if for parting:

> *White in the moon the long road lies*
> *That leads me from my love,*

yet more for meeting:

> *How sad and mad and bad it was!*
> *But then, how it was sweet!*

Lane

YOU WILL NOT FIND MULBERRY trees growing wild, nor often medlars. Both are the choice of keen and well-to-do gardeners; Shakespeare certainly knew the medlar. The 'black' mulberry was introduced around London in the late sixteenth century - the first in Syon Park in 1548 - with a view to producing English silk, the 'white' variety, which silkworms prefer, being not yet known. However, silk weaving became a cottage industry for a short time, and it was said that every parson was encouraged to plant a tree. It is hardy: 'here we go round the mulberry bush on a cold and frosty morning'! and is very long-living, and many an old vicarage has one to this day. Birds and appetites permitting, the juicy fruits should not be eaten till they are darkest crimson, and then immediately. ¶ The medlar is a rather crab-bed, angular tree, whose curious fruit, like a small squat brown pear, has an unusually large and decorative calyx where the flower has been. It falls when hard and still green, to make an excellent jelly. But the epicure keeps it till it is rust-coloured and 'sleepy', when he will pronounce it ambrosial.

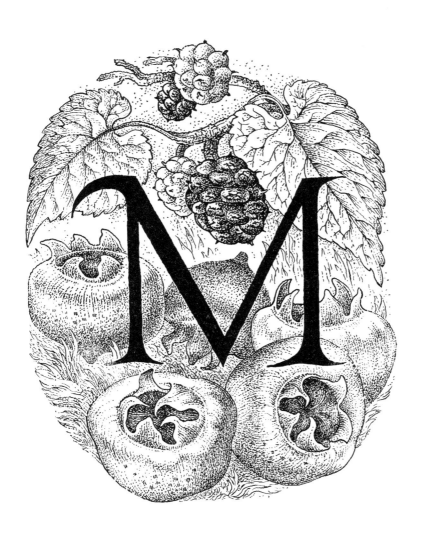

Medlar, Mulberry

35

'NETTLE-CREEPER' IS THE COUNTRY name for the whitethroat. Other birds have their familiar names - ousel, throstle, yaffle; Jenny Wren, Tom Tit, Magpie and Robin of course, and less known 'spadgy' for sparrow. But 'nettle-creeper' betrays that this is ('was', one now hopes) a birds'-nesting name. Bare-kneed small boys know dodges to avoid the stings, from which caterpillars feeding on the leaves (red admiral, peacock and others) are protected by their own stiff hairs. Conscientious ecologists however need not grow nettles, handsome plants though they are, expressly for caterpillars, nor for their other uses, as a dye, as the fibre of textile and paper, or as a delicious spring vegetable, for so far ejected are their innumerable seeds and so far-reaching, down and sideways, their tough yellow roots that they soon colonise. The new agriculture has given them an additional habitat in the unreachable no-man's-land between over-low hedge and new barbed-wire fence. ¶ However, the nettle-creeping whitethroat's sweet sharp gabble is heard less and less. A ground nest may escape cuckoos but must have many hazards.

Nest of the Nettle Creeper (Whitethroat) among Nettles

37

IT IS TYPICAL OF US TO CONSIDER
the oak a peculiarly British tree - 'Hearts of oak are our ships' - not knowing that there are 230 species, of which but two are native, *Quercus robur* ('English', peduncu-late) and *Quercus petraea* ('Durmast', sessile), according to whether their acorns have or have not stalks. Another oak flourishes in this country, the handsome Turkey oak, with smaller more indented leaves, and acorn cups covered with green bristles, as if it had crossed with a Spanish chestnut. ¶ The English oak is our most characteristic tree, and must be the easiest to identify - by its low-domed crown and wriggling branches, its wavy-edged leaves and egg-in-eggcup fruits, its galls ready for oak-apple day on May 29th, its rich colours, mustard yellow of catkin and copper of young leaf in May, russet in autumn. Most re-markable is its huge girth in advanced old age, as in Moccas Park in Herefordshire, immortalised by Francis Kilvert's Diary (April 22, 1876): 'No human hand set those oaks. They are "the trees which the Lord hath planted". They look as if they had been at the beginning and making of the world, and they will probably see its end.'

Turkey Oak   Durmast or Sessile Oak   English Oak
(Quercus cerris) (Quercus petræa) (Quercus robur)

WHY DID VICTORIANA SO PROLI-
ferate with pincushions? square and fat, covered with
crochet or trimmed with pillowlace, studded with 'Wel-
come Little Stranger' for a new baby; pocket size and
thin, in the shape of star, fan, heart; or clampable to the
table, the habit of sewing tackle being to fall to the floor
and disappear. ¶ Are Jane and Ann Taylor's *Original
Poems for Infant Minds* (1804) responsible? In *The Pin*,
'little heedless Emily's' punishment for leaving a pin on
the floor was to miss a ride to see an air balloon. But
cautionary tales should anticipate children's reactions to
such needless cruelty:

> *The carriage rattled to the door,*
> *Then rattled fast away.*
> *Poor Emily! she was not in,*
> *For want of just a single pin.*

'Poor Emily' indeed; In the time she was cutting her
pincushion in two, could not Mamma have put a stitch
in her pelisse? or better, could she not have noticed before-
hand that it was pinless? She had 'plenty more' even then
- and made sure to have enough in future.

Primrose, Pot, Pincushion, Pins, Pillow lace

THIS LETTER, WITH ENCIRCLING crown and long train, is a fitting capital for 'Queen'. Calligraphers love it. ¶ The Quince, rare, large and golden, deserves such an opening letter. It is the aroma that is supreme, unequalled (like that of coffee) even by its taste when made into clear ruby-red jelly – for there is nothing sharper than the iron-hard fruit itself. It must be left about for as long as possible, impregnating all the air around, and good to look upon as well, a brown star-shape ornamenting its rounded top, a soft bloom rubbing off its yellow surface. ¶ The star is all that remains of the flower. Unlike those of the kindred apple and pear (the word 'Quince' is a corruption of 'Cydonian' pear), they grow singly on the tree, which can be temperamental, liking a well-drained sheltered position. But insufficient quinces can be eked out with 'japonica' quinces, smaller, darker gold and even more acid if possible, but coming a close second in scent and flavour.

Quince 　　　 'Japanese Quince'
(Cydonia oblonga)　(Chænomeles japonica)

CAN ANY LETTER REPRESENT MORE sounds? trilled by Scot and Italian, vibrated in the uvula in France, rolled round the tongue in rural Wessex and in America, slurred by babies, while the rest of us scarcely pronounce it. ¶ But to the drawing. Now that corn is cut, threshed and baled by combine harvester, ricks with their finials, staddles and all have disappeared from the farmyard. No farm hand would hanker after flailing for hours in the cross-draught of a threshing floor, but even though the rick must be re-opened in a few months he never thought the thatching wasted labour, nor making the finial, which must include full heads of corn. To propitiate the birds? More likely because it was always done, the origin in fertility rites long forgotten; certainly because the skills of shaping with the self-twisting knot, and of plaiting with long supple straw that had never known chemical fertilisers, were enjoyed, each locality or even each farm perpetuating its pattern of bird, ball, spire or crown, that we now see only prettified in the tourist shops.

Rick ornaments

45

'HOW SWEET IS THE SHEPHERD'S SWEET lot!' Is it? The Arcadian picture of pipe-playing and garland-making hardly fits a Gabriel Oak, out in all weathers, unpaid vet and farm hand, about any job from midwifery to de-maggoting. ¶ The Shepherd's 'gear, tackle and trim' perpetuates crafts other than his own. His crook, combining the skills of smith and walkingstick-maker, was designed to grip without injury. The bell whose 'drowsy tinklings lull the distant folds' might carry the proud signature of the famous church bell founder, Robert Wells of Aldbourne. His smock was probably made by his wife in the ordinary course of a day's work. Its design was inevitable, being an adaptation of the shirt or chemise worn day and night by both sexes. It must be ample enough to cover his only working suit to knees and wrists, yet be easily pulled on either way, the elastic smocking keeping the garment from falling forward. Was the 'box' embroidery essential? Perhaps, if on hiring days the feather-stitched circles suggested shepherds' crooks; but necessary it was - for the satisfaction of the needlewoman.

Smock, Shepherds' crooks, Sheep bells

47

WHEN WE WERE CHILDREN STILL small enough to need grown-up assistance in fastening our many back buttons, my mother would sometimes put us into the big bed still cosy from her warmth, and to keep us occupied till she was ready would provide us with 'the Treasure Box'. Though we lifted the lid a hundred times, new every morning was our love for both container and contents, which we would draw out slowly one by one as though from a Christmas stocking. The first peep revealed a length of tatted lace, that would make necklace or crown. All round the edges the box was encrusted with painted top shells in their undercoat of mother-of-pearl, small cowries, mussels and scallops filling the centres; but the strong temptation to dislodge them had been diverted by the provision within of graspable specimens - striped whelk, frail cockle, and a prettily marked limpet lying in the last cup, star-spotted at the rim, from our dolls' tea-set. At the bottom of the box rolled the 'jewels': pinless brooches and prized hatpin tops, that made us look covetously at lady guests removing their headgear on arrival. Beads awaited reunion with their necklaces in a china trinket box painted with roses, which I have to this day. ¶ When a little older we made treasure boxes of our own, competitively similar, lining them with cottonwool which would receive kindly our patterns of shells, beads - and hatpin tops, unlawfully obtained.

Tea cup, Trinkets, a child's Treasures, Tatting

49

WE WERE LOOKING FOR A WILTSHIRE hoop-raved waggon, but never thought we should come upon anything like this one. If thus in old age, what can it have been when in double harness it rode the rutted white lanes and the harvested stubblefields? ¶ Surely never was waggon more richly ornamented. There was not a member - and most of them remained - but had its bevel, chamfer, beading, scoop or scallop. The sign-writing still showed the date, 1851. An exquisite example of the farm smock had appeared in the Great Exhibition; this decoration too might almost be called embroidery. ¶ But 'decoration' and 'ornament' are misnomers, implying the unnecessary: this work of the drawshave was functional - essential to reduce the weight without impairing the strength. Here is part of the undercarriage, whose function was that of 'suspension' in today's car, those beautiful cotton-reel spindles doing the work of springs. ¶ The waggon should have been in a museum. But none could give it such a setting, framed in its open byre that looked out over as yet unravaged fields and hedges, and embowered in creamy umbels of hogweed and wild carrot.

Under-carriage of waggon, in Undergrowth, with
Umbelliferous plants

51

ST VALENTINE'S PRETTY NAME IS fortunate to be associated with the tuning-up of bird-song; St Francis should have been allotted February 14th instead of October 4th. In *A Midsummer Night's Dream* Theseus greets the two pairs of disentangled lovers with 'Goodmorrow, friends. St Valentine is past. Begin these lovebirds but to couple now?' ¶ In third-century Rome the February festival of Juno was celebrated by drawing lots for lovers. Christianity tried to substitute saints, but the old custom stuck. ¶ Pepys writes in 1677: 'This morning came up to my wife's bedside . . . little Will Mercer to be her Valentine; and brought her name writ upon blue paper in gold letters, done by himself, very pretty . . .' He alludes to lot-drawing: 'Find that Mrs Pierce's little girl is my Valentine, having drawn me . . . I do observe the fashion of drawing of Mottos as well as names . . . My wife's was "Most virtuous and most fair".' ¶ The valentine kept up the tradition of a game not to be taken seriously (like Bathsheba Everdene's). 'Had a valentine sent me with 2d. to pay but didn't take it in' runs a boy's diary in 1883. But on Feb. 14 the following year he was sending snowdrops to the girl who became his wife.

Valentine with Violets

53

THE WORD 'WELL' CALLS UP ROM-
antic memories – of Biblical wells where women drew
water for camels; of the wishing wells of childhood and
the game of 'Ghost at the Well'; of the princess who
dropped her ball into the water and the frog prince who
found it; of lucky wells full of coins it would be unlucky
to retrieve; of holy saints' wells that could heal all dis-
eases. ¶ Each cottage usually had its own, conveniently
near the door, and protectively walled about, with a
thatched cover to the winch whose bucket, lowered to
sufficient depth, made a good refrigerator. The commun-
al well, rendezvous of the village, was shielded from sun
and weather by a conical or square stone-tiled roof sup-
ported by wooden arches. ¶ Today there are still many
who yearn for well water, but it was in the nightmare
drought of 1976, when forest trees defoliated and the
Thames began to run backwards, that any wells remain-
ing really came into their own, for even then few ran dry.
One lucky woman found she had one under her kitchen
table – and kept it dark.

Well-windlass, Well-head, Winch, Wall, Woodland

R: What do we do about 'X'? H: Leave it out. It has no business in our alphabet. *R: Still, it's there; we must do something.* H: You can't draw Xerxes or Xantippe or X-rays. *R: Let's go through the dictionary.* H: Xylophone! *R: That's only a board and metal tubes.* H: An old alphabet here does Xmas for 'X'. *R: Ugh! You know I can't bear Xmas for Christmas!* H: You needn't do camels and mangers – you could do robins and holly, stars and bells, Christmas trees . . . *R: Well, I won't. It isn't ME!* H: Some alphabets lump 'X', 'Y' and 'Z' with Ampersand. *R: That's cheating. Besides, I've done 'Y'. Oh!!! In Bentham and Hooker! A plant beginning with X! Xanthium!* H: Never heard of it. Besides, that's the Latin name. *That's* cheating. *R: It's got an English name; your grandfather's written 'Cockleburr' beside it, and when he found it.* H: But *you've* never found it? *R: Yes, once; in a cornfield.* H: You're making it up. (*Reads*). 'Introduced from America.' *R: It's in Sowerby. Look!* H: I can't say it looks any better than groundsel. *R: I like groundsel!* H: That's not the point. I've never seen a Xanthium in a cornfield, and shouldn't like it if I had. *R: No plant is dislikable. And I'm going to draw* two *kinds of* Xanthium. H: You can make anything likable. But I can't write 200 words on a plant I don't know. 'It's not M E!'

Xanthium spinosum   Xanthium strumarium
(Spiny cocklebur)   *(Cocklebur or Burweed)*

57

A THOUSAND YEARS AGO NEARLY all our words now beginning with 'y' began with 'g'. Are we gentler? Hardly! Lazier? Probably; yet the Welsh, who have vocalised the 'y' sound entirely, are certainly not lazier still. 'Y' occupies only four pages of the Shorter Oxford Dictionary, giving the artist little choice except in 'yellow', of which in the plant world there is plenty. As a general (and often broken) rule, white flowers bloom first, when light is scarce, then yellow; blues and reds following later. Yellow Rattle of the meadow, downland Yellow-wort and woodland Yellow Pimpernel are not early flowers. Yarrow is both early and late, and its ubiquity must have helped its use as first aid kit in staunching blood. It is tempting to derive its very name from the Anglo-Saxon word for 'ready to hand' - our 'gear'. ❡ Yew was sacred before there were churches, but when its wood became essential for bow-making the churchyard could provide an arsenal conveniently out of the reach of cattle easily poisoned by yew leaves and berries.

Yellow wort, Yarrow, Yellow Rattle, Yellow pimpernel, Yew

'Z' IS A VOICED 'S' TURNED THE OTHER way round, zigzagging like a buzzing insect. Does not 'zither' sound like a plucked string? ¶ Zither, cittern, guitar, all have the same root but are by no means the same instrument, though all are adaptations of the ancient 'psaltery', familiar through that magical refrain in the story of the Three Holy Children who at 'the sound of the cornet, flute, harp, sackbut, psaltery, dulcimer' refused to 'fall down and worship the golden image that Nebuchadnezzar the king had set up'. ¶ The German zither, small and light, to lie on lap or table, is an ideal solo instrument, since both air and accompaniment can be played on its thirty strings. Traditionally it is Tyrolean, suggesting ethereal mountain airs rather than 'the lascivious pleasing of a lute' or the passion that can 'hale souls out of men's bodies' - allusions reminding us that it was in Shakespeare's time that plucked strings had their heyday.

Zither

61

from

The Old Stile Press

88

The printing of this book was completed in
August, 1984 by Nicolas McDowall at
The Old Stile Press, 32, St. John's Park,
Blackheath, London, Great Britain.

The type, 16 point Poliphilus with Blado, was set at
The Whittington Press, Gloucestershire.

The paper is Zerkall mould made. ❡ The blocks
were made by Swains. ❡ All copies were bound by
Smith Settle, Otley, Yorkshire.

Of the Main Edition, 160 numbered copies are for sale.

The 26 lettered copies of the Special Edition
have an additional two-page spread
and pulls of all the blocks
contained in a portfolio.

❡

£45